POP CHARTS

First published in Great Britain in 2008 by Cassell Illustrated,
an imprint of Octopus Publishing Group Ltd,
2–4 Heron Quays, London E14 4JP

An Hachette Livre company
www.hachettelivre.co.uk

Reprinted in 2009 (twice) by Cassell Illustrated

A CIP catalogue record for this book is available from the
British Library.

ISBN-13: 978-1-844-03664-6

Production: Caroline Alberti
Commissioning Editor: Laura Price
Publisher: Mathew Clayton

Printed and bound in China

10 9 8 7 6 5 4 3

With sincere thanks for all the gags to:

Lewis Coghlin, Paul Copperwaite, Carl Lyons,
Rhodri Marsden, Laura Price, Fiona Kellagher,
Ruth Patrick, Andrew Taylor, Mark Scott,
Sarah Hammerton, Mathew Clayton,
Jane Smith, Fiona Smith,
Lucy Avery, Daniel Jenkins

Floyd's Summer Term Timetable

Mon	Maths	Physics	RE	Music	French	History	English
Tues	History	Biology	Maths	Maths	English	Art	Art
Wed	Maths	English	Geo-graphy	Geo-graphy	Games	Games	Games
Thur	English	History	Dark Sarcasm cancelled	Dark Sarcasm cancelled	Biology	Maths	German
Fri	Physics	PE	Maths	English	French	Gen Studies	Gen Studies

Paranoia Assessment

When you're in love with a beautiful woman...

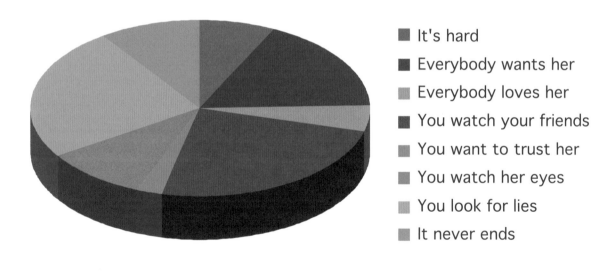

- It's hard
- Everybody wants her
- Everybody loves her
- You watch your friends
- You want to trust her
- You watch her eyes
- You look for lies
- It never ends

Probability of being loved (by anyone)

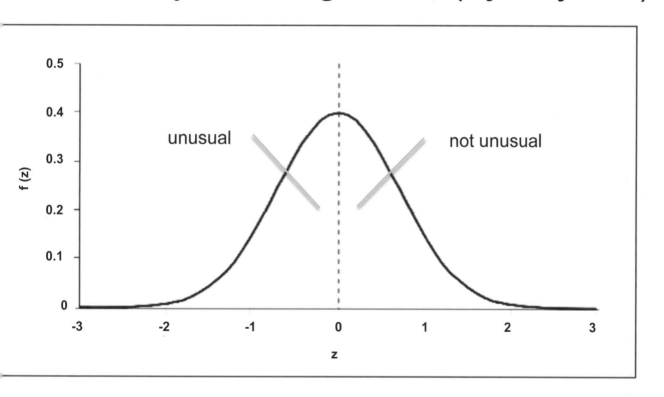

Defining qualities of showgirls at the Copacabana (the hottest spot north of Havana)

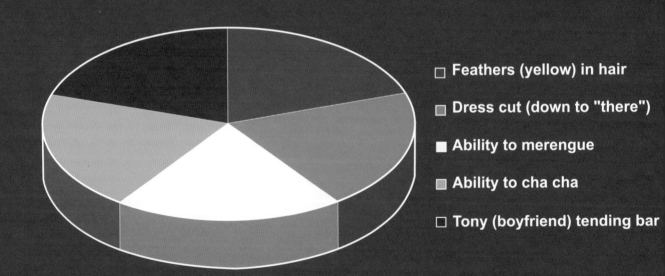

- Feathers (yellow) in hair
- Dress cut (down to "there")
- Ability to merengue
- Ability to cha cha
- Tony (boyfriend) tending bar

Your personalised schedule at the YMCA

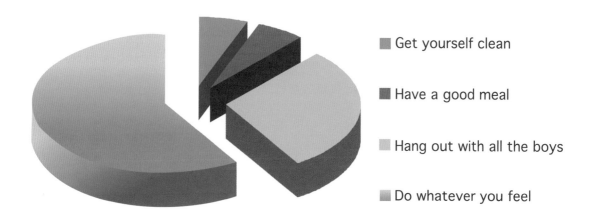

- Get yourself clean
- Have a good meal
- Hang out with all the boys
- Do whatever you feel

Kinks mid-year assessment

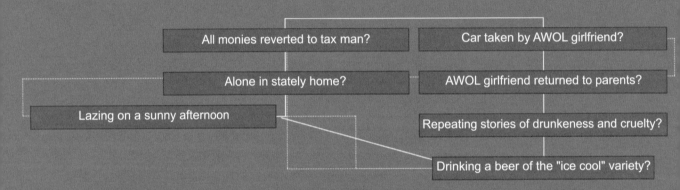

Likelihood of occupations for Mr D L Roth

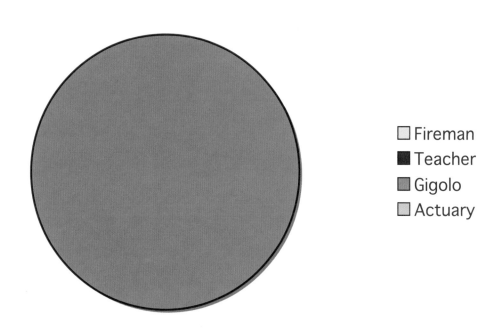

- ☐ Fireman
- ■ Teacher
- ■ Gigolo
- ☐ Actuary

Potential reduction in quality of blackness over time – Visage

Direction of fade

Data summary of headgear and relative erotic attraction

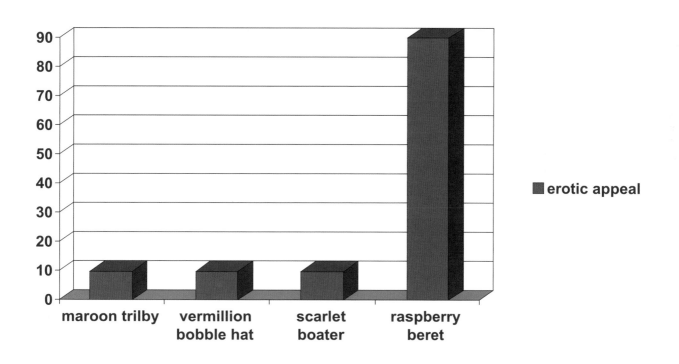

Relationship between "rhythm" as a "dancer" and seriousness of common health complaints

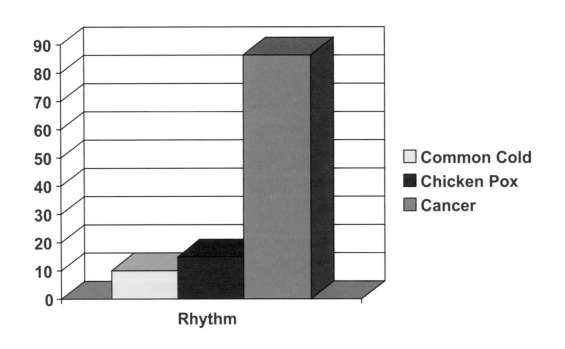

Dating Questionnaire

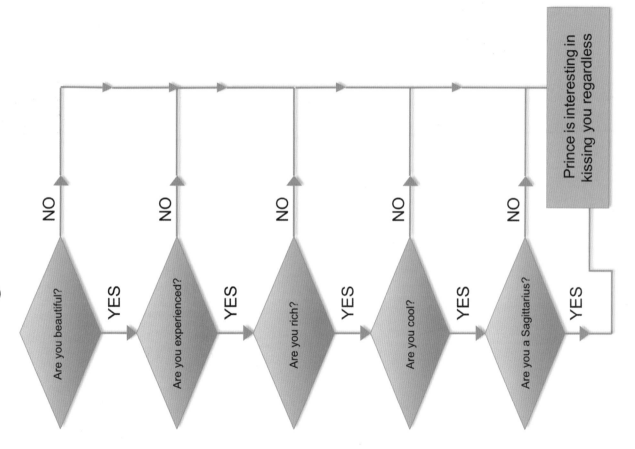

Organization chart for passing on of information within the business model

- Invoices – pass on to bought ledger

- Contracts – pass on to legal

- Purchase Orders – pass on to accounts

- The Dutchie – pass on the left-hand side

Advance celebration planning strategy over time

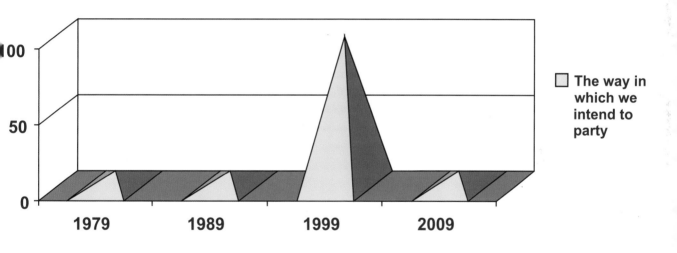

- 100
- 50
- 0

1979 1989 1999 2009

☐ The way in which we intend to party

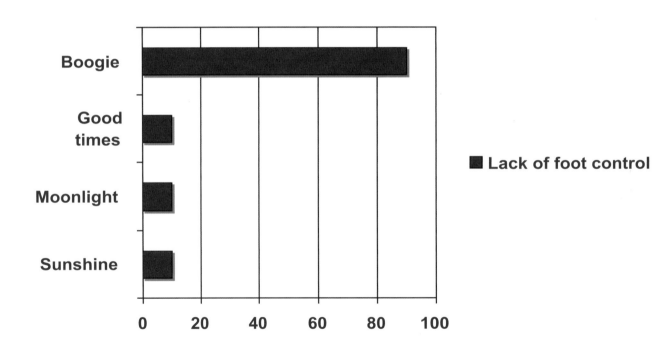

Agnetha Fältskog's preparation for imminent visitor arrival

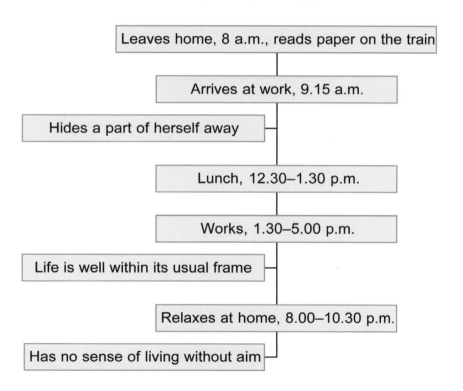

Bush/Floyd light paucity in other sidedness

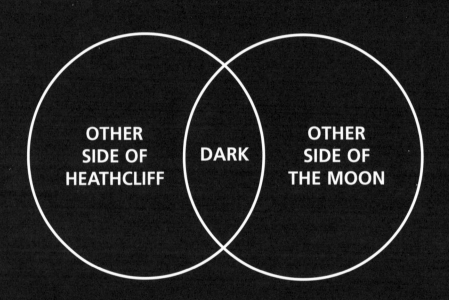

% probability of being over the rainbow

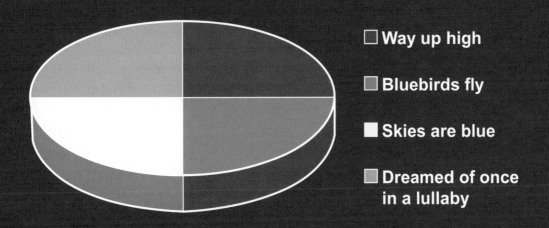

- Way up high
- Bluebirds fly
- Skies are blue
- Dreamed of once in a lullaby

Mortality rates and causes in the radio broadcast sector

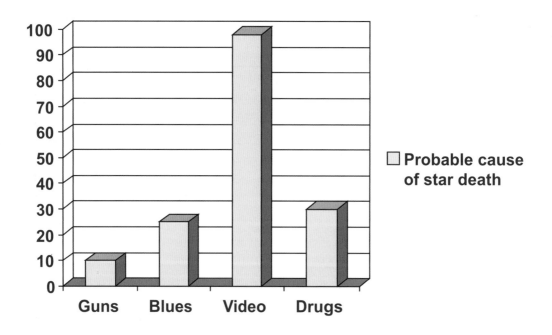

Preferred gait selection by style of walk

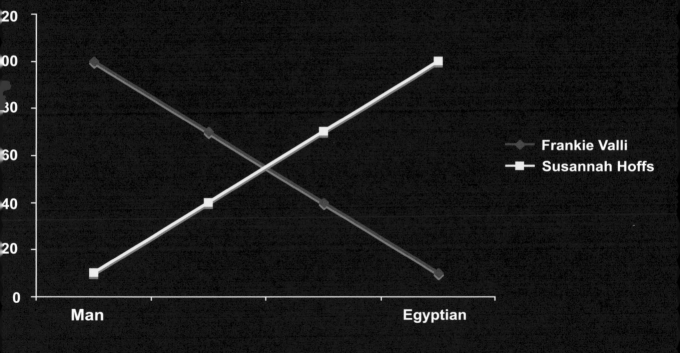

Gibb oxygen intake cause and effect

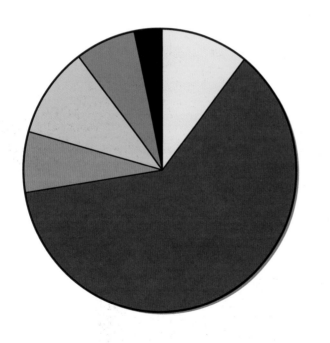

- ☐ Woman
- ■ More than a woman
- ■ Clinically obese
- ☐ Less than a woman
- ■ Primate and lesser species
- ■ Achondroplastic

Aretha Franklin's modus operandi for a reverent petition

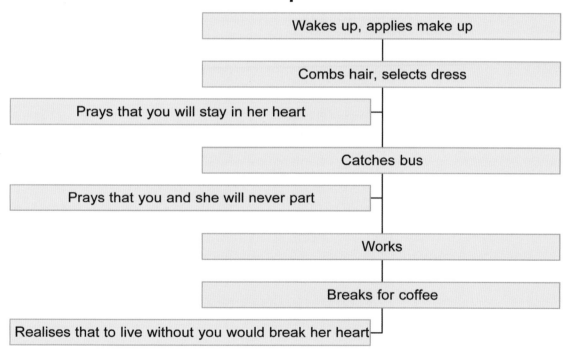

Available services offered – Club Tropicana

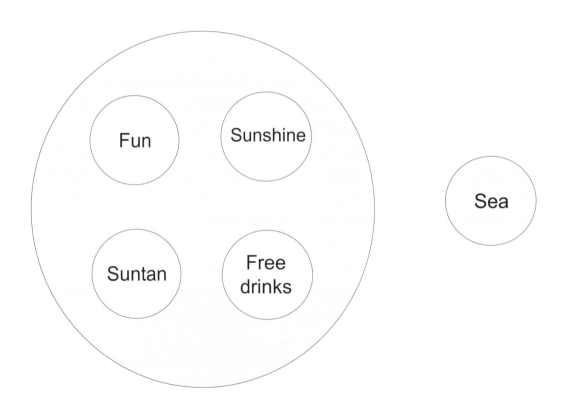

Data review of personal proximity and relative avian appearance

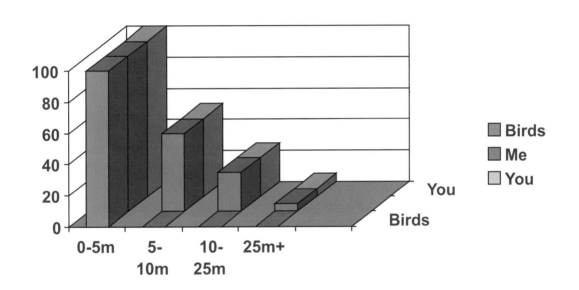

Source: Carpenters

Rabbit check list by noticeable traits

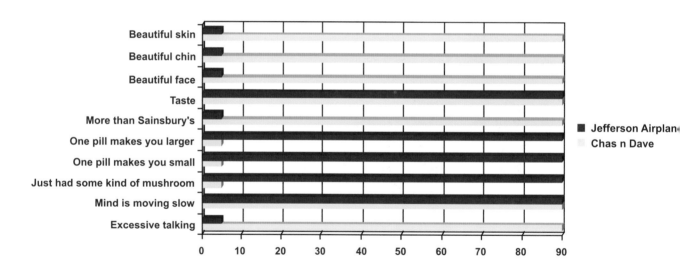

Assessment of those whom Beelzebub has put the devil aside for

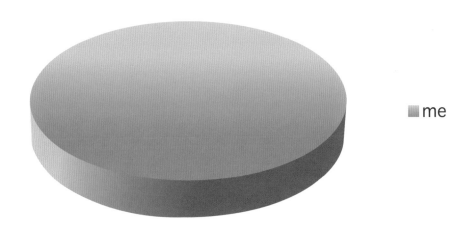

me

Quick guide to establishing relationships

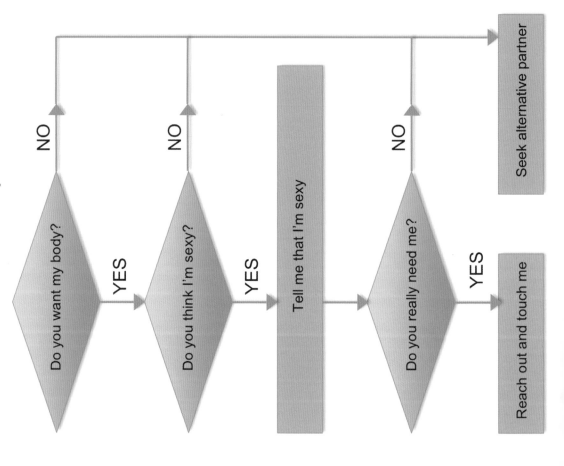

Do you want my body?

YES

NO

Do you think I'm sexy?

YES

NO

Tell me that I'm sexy

Do you really need me?

YES

NO

Reach out and touch me

Seek alternative partner

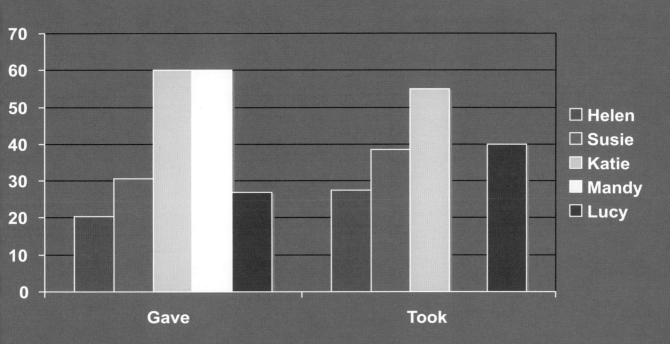

Degree of taking on donation given

Source: B Manilow

Comparative weights of metals and family members

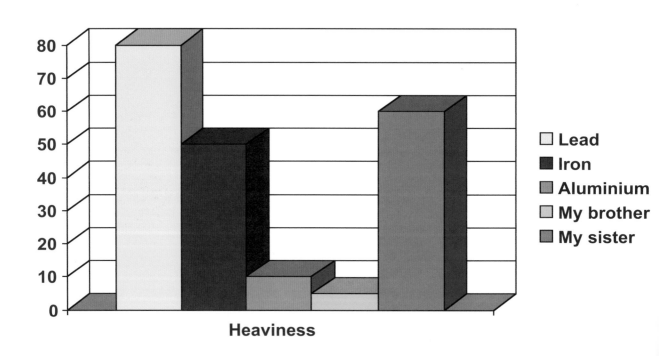

Alternative amorous attention of Mr R Williams for celestial bodies

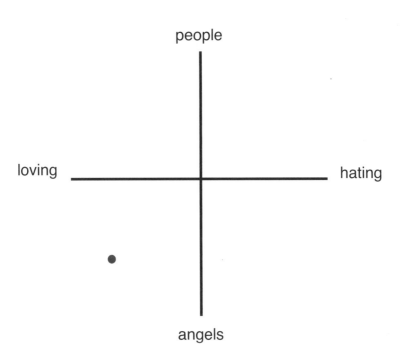

Causes of increased incendiary effects not initiated by us

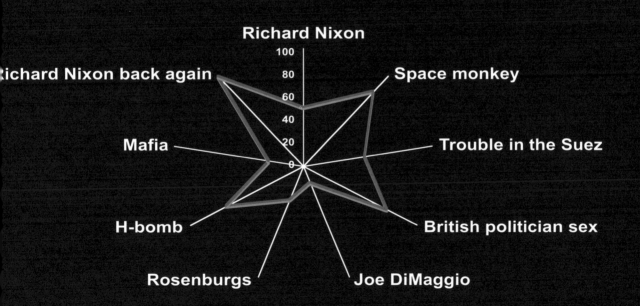

— Burning fire

Richard Nixon back again — Richard Nixon — Space monkey

Mafia — Trouble in the Suez

H-bomb — British politician sex

Rosenburgs — Joe DiMaggio

Source: Billy Joel

Chance of sourcing amorous attachment

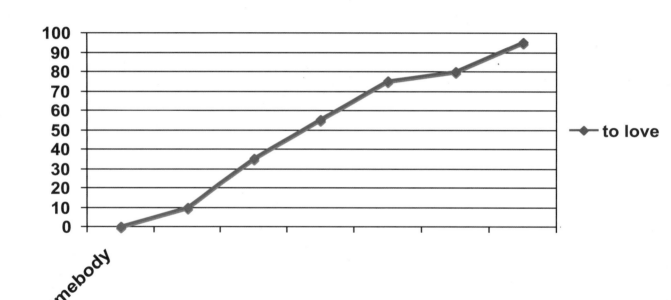

Love Potion quality scores

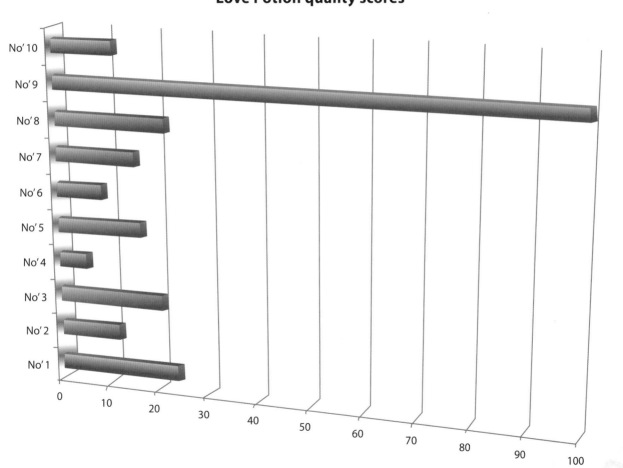

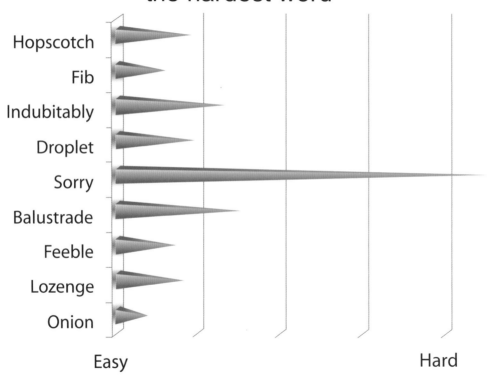

Survey to determine what seems to be the hardest word

| | Easy | | | | Hard |

- Hopscotch
- Fib
- Indubitably
- Droplet
- Sorry
- Balustrade
- Feeble
- Lozenge
- Onion

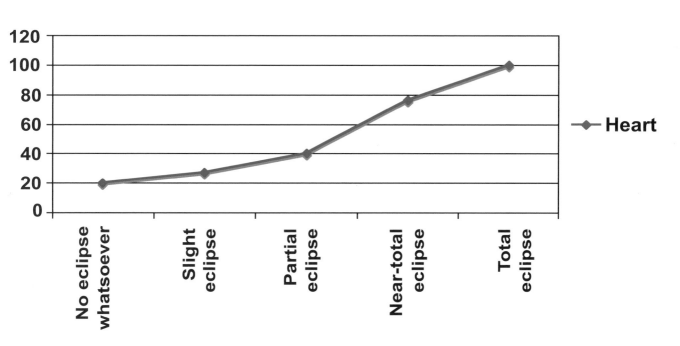

Probability of percussive phenomena by location

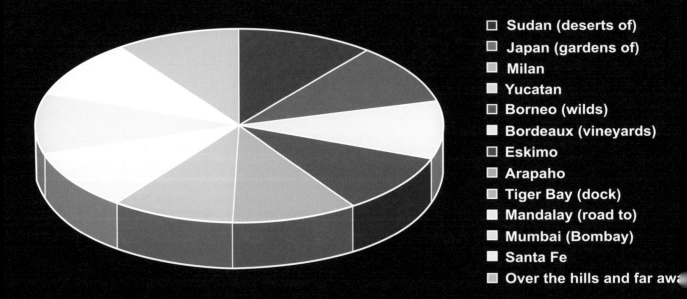

- ☐ Sudan (deserts of)
- ☐ Japan (gardens of)
- ☐ Milan
- ☐ Yucatan
- ☐ Borneo (wilds)
- ☐ Bordeaux (vineyards)
- ☐ Eskimo
- ☐ Arapaho
- ☐ Tiger Bay (dock)
- ☐ Mandalay (road to)
- ☐ Mumbai (Bombay)
- ☐ Santa Fe
- ☐ Over the hills and far awa

Source: I Dury

Guidance For Tourists

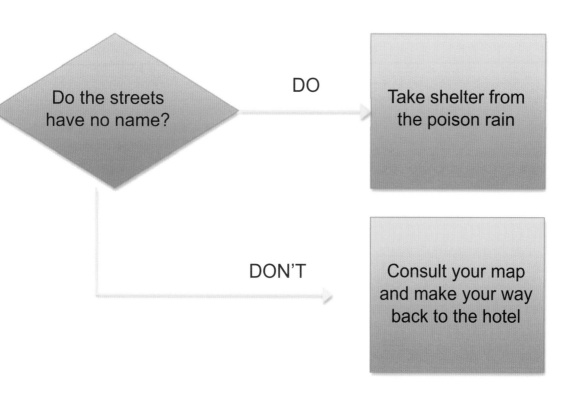

Achievements and Goals

- Things so far achieved:

  Coming a long long way together

  Through hard times

  And Good

- Future Goals and Steps

  Celebrate you Baby

  Praise you as I should

Source: F. B. Slim

Good years by content

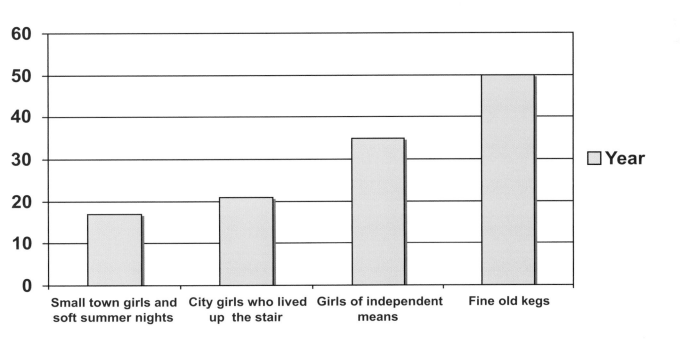

Source: F Sinatra

De Niro linguistic spread while waiting

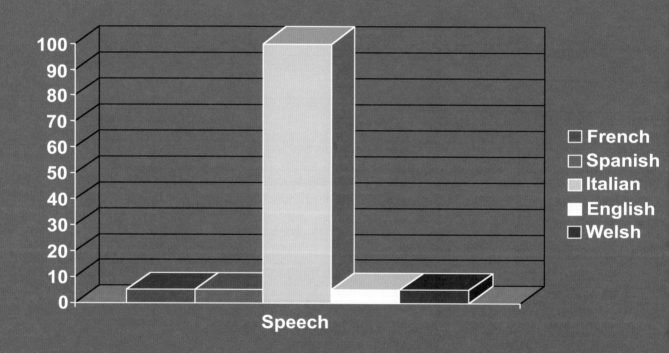

US states on the mind of Mr Raymond Charles

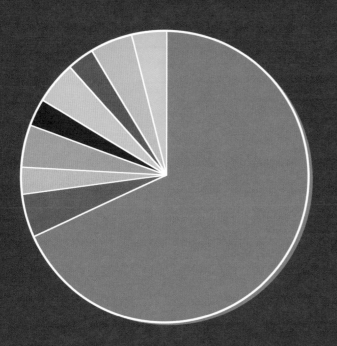

- Georgia
- Alaska
- New Jersey
- Tennessee
- Utah
- Florida
- Iowa
- Maine
- Hawaii

% of lunar surface seen

(sample: those reaching too high, too far, too soon)

- Whole
- Some
- None

Source: The Waterbo

Worldwide countdown assessment by area

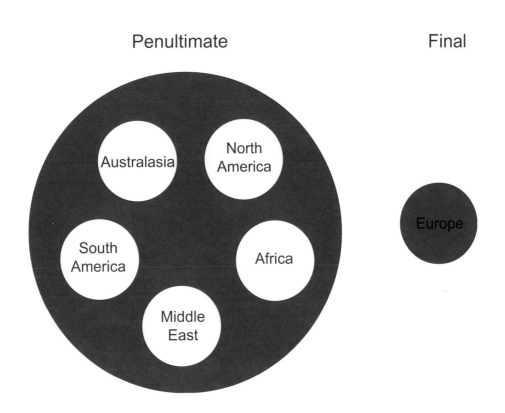

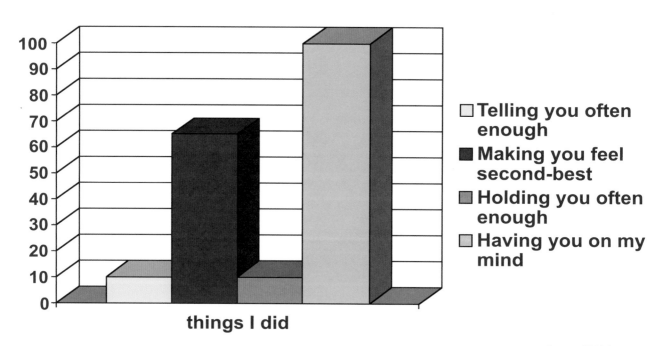

Degree of time spent on you

things I did

- Telling you often enough
- Making you feel second-best
- Holding you often enough
- Having you on my mind

Source: W Nelson

Chief elements of evenings dedicated to females

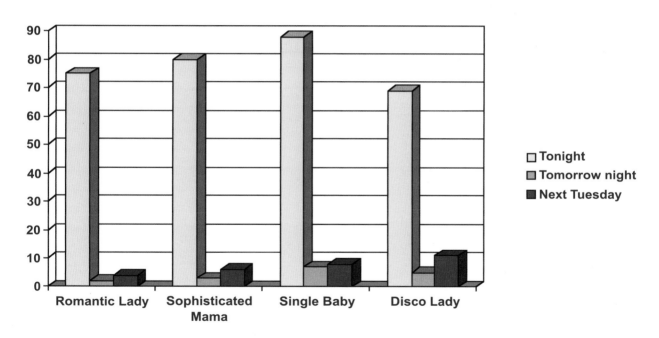

Source: Kool and the Gang

Blur partner selection sequence for paranoid love in the nineties

Females who are males

Who like males to be females

Who do males like they're females

Who do females like they're males

Always should be
someone you really love

Hollywood/News/Rush Love-Power ratio

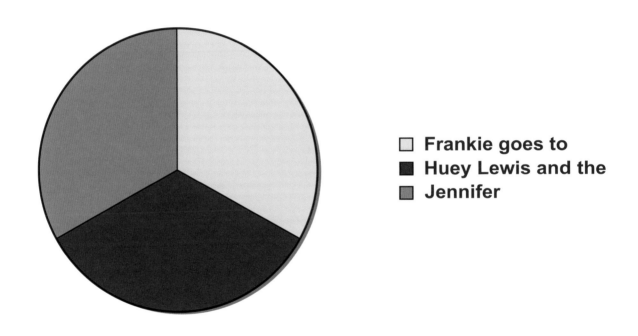

☐ **Frankie goes to**
■ **Huey Lewis and the**
■ **Jennifer**

Breakdown of assets and attributes for future financial reward potential

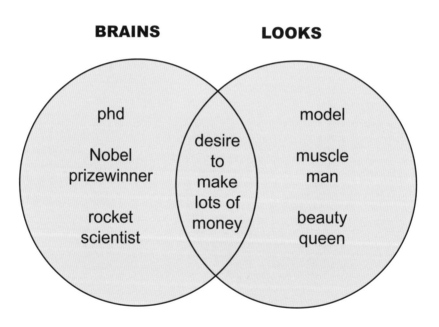

Reason's for unwitting hurting and causation of weeping

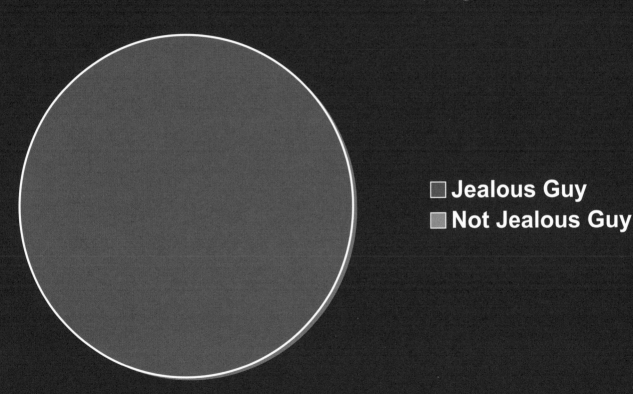

☐ Jealous Guy
▨ Not Jealous Guy

The ones who tried to reach me and relative successes

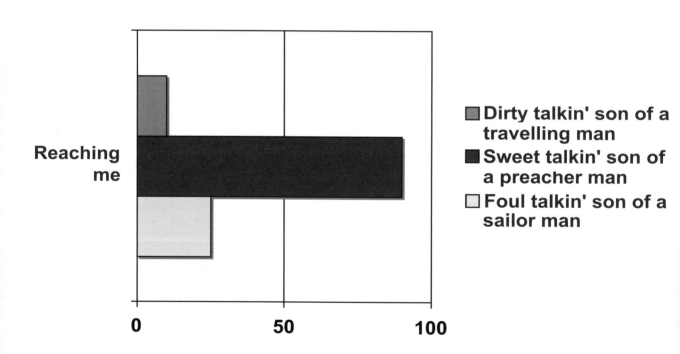

Marley tears-to-females relationship

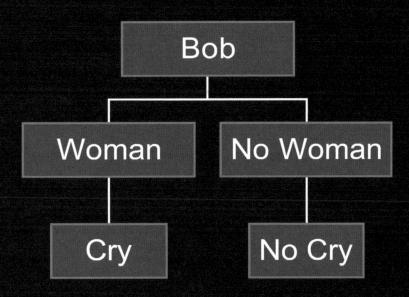

Ways that Mr M Bolton is supposed to live without you

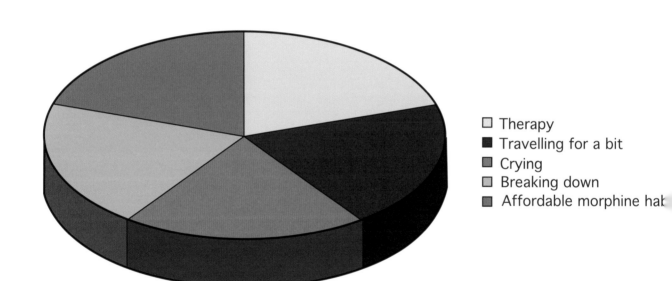

- ☐ Therapy
- ■ Travelling for a bit
- ▨ Crying
- ▨ Breaking down
- ▨ Affordable morphine hab

% cause of having both "a good time" and "a ball" with Mr F Mercury

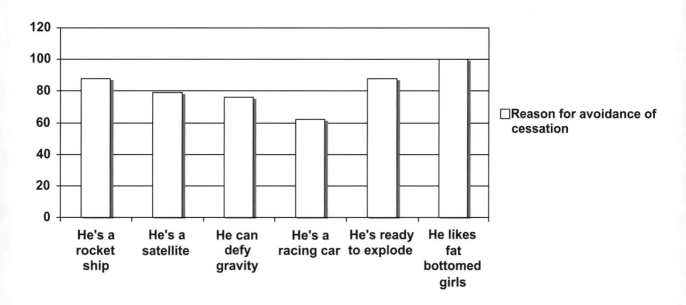

Final analysis of positive outcome resulting from conflict

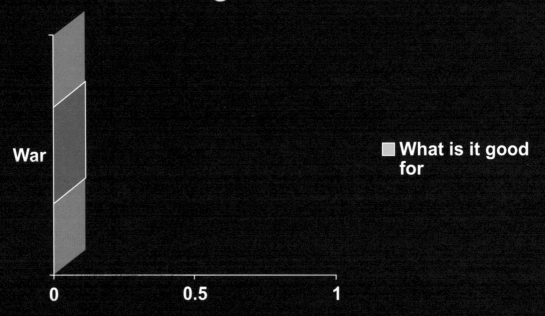

Areas of uncertainty regarding Yuletide awareness

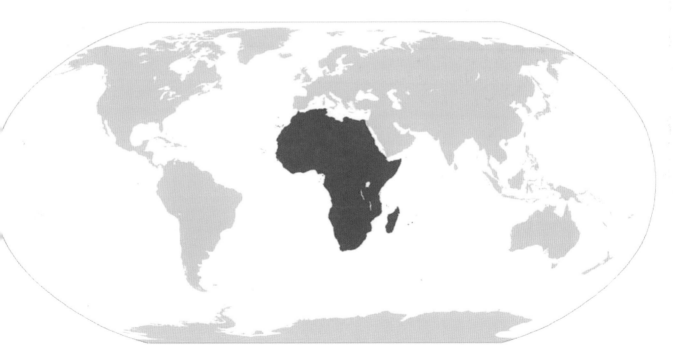

Source: BandAid

Assistance in determining whether it's worth placing a call to Ghostbusters

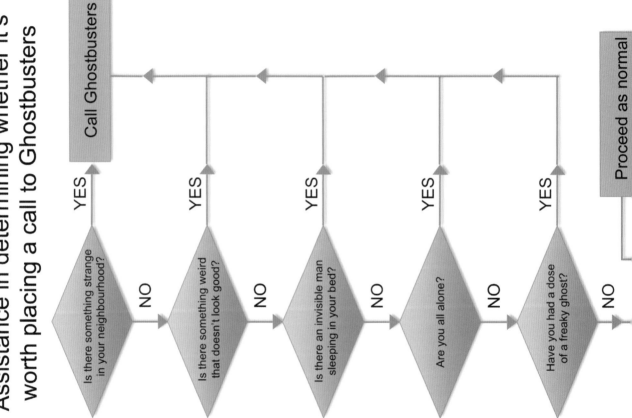

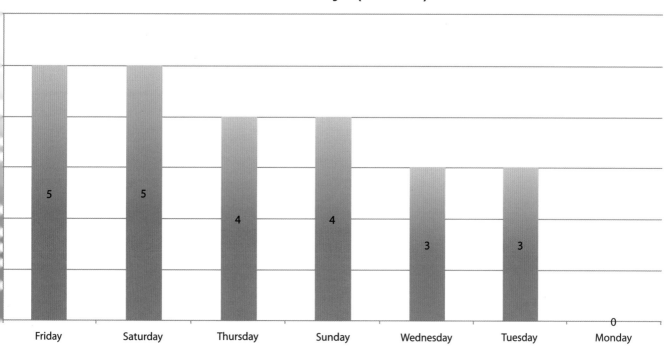

Favourite days (out of 5)

Friday	Saturday	Thursday	Sunday	Wednesday	Tuesday	Monday
5	5	4	4	3	3	0

Source: Boomtown Rats

ELVIS/IGGY PREFERENCE OF ANIMAL AMBITION IN RELATION TO PARTNER

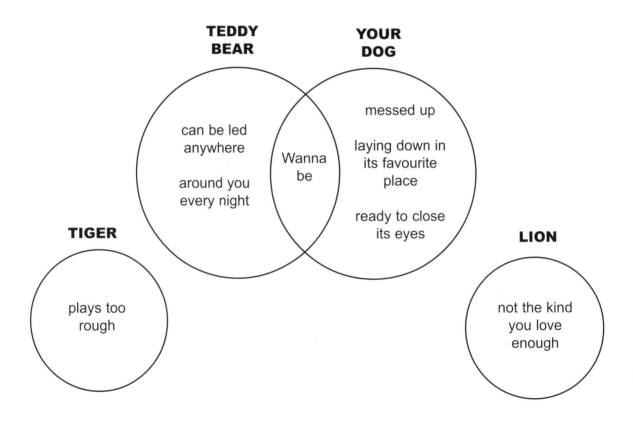

TEDDY BEAR

YOUR DOG

TIGER

LION

can be led anywhere

around you every night

Wanna be

messed up

laying down in its favourite place

ready to close its eyes

plays too rough

not the kind you love enough

Ways of discerning potential machines of physical congress

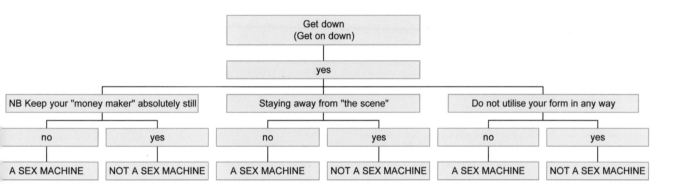

Things Meatloaf would do for love

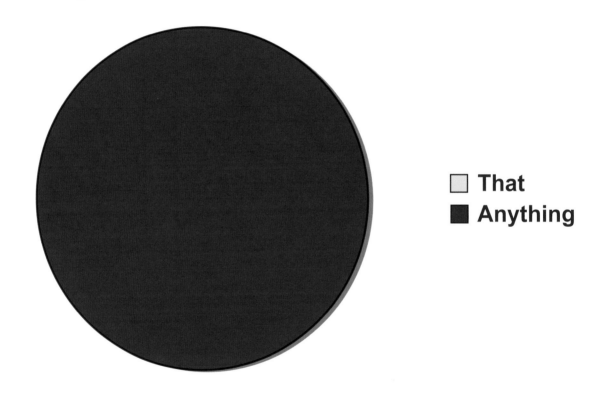

☐ That
■ Anything

Degrees of fly – super vs. pretty for a white guy

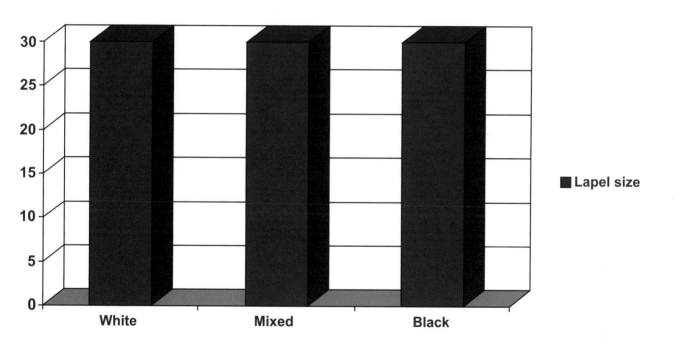

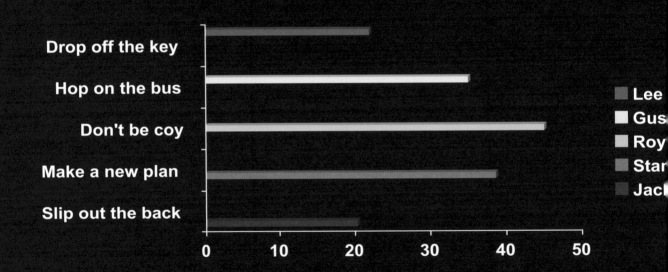

Ways to leave your lover

Drop off the key	
Hop on the bus	
Don't be coy	
Make a new plan	
Slip out the back	

0   10   20   30   40   50

Lee
Gus
Roy
Star
Jack

Areas of reported rocking

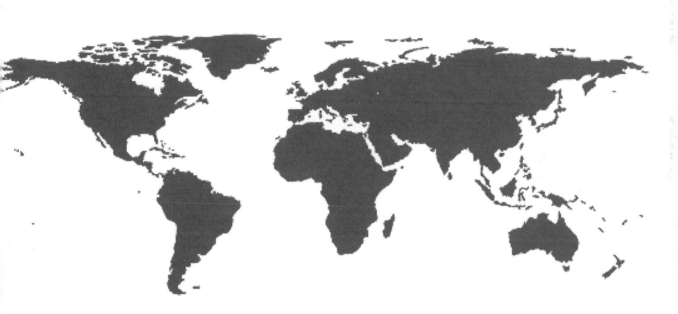

Leading pointers of proximity to Paradise City

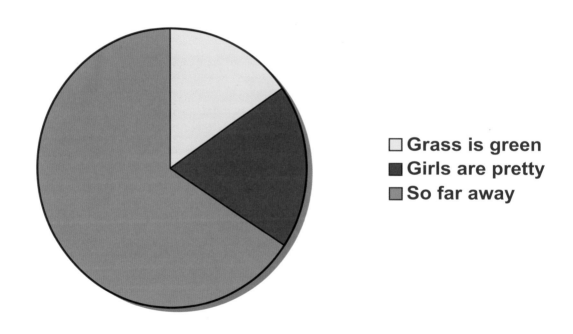

☐ Grass is green
■ Girls are pretty
☐ So far away

Discussion group topic spread
– popular music

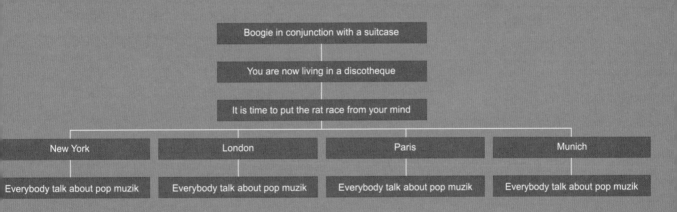

Boogie in conjunction with a suitcase

You are now living in a discotheque

It is time to put the rat race from your mind

New York	London	Paris	Munich
Everybody talk about pop muzik	Everybody talk about pop muzik	Everybody talk about pop muzik	Everybody talk about pop muzik

Source: M

Probability of things only getting better

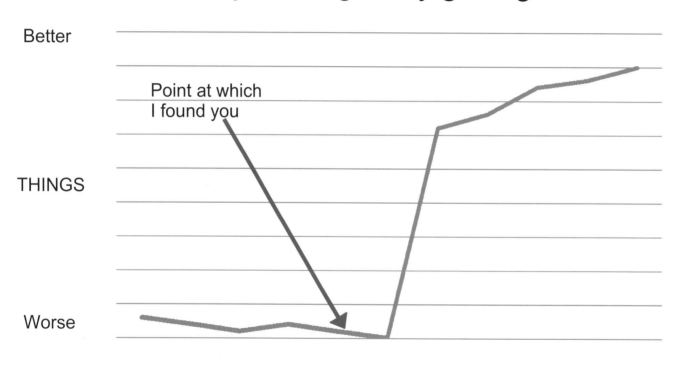

Fruits I'll eat when I move to the country (qty)

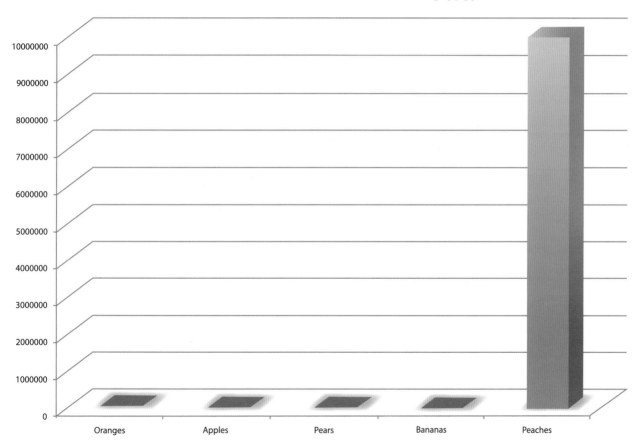

Source: Presidents of the United States of America

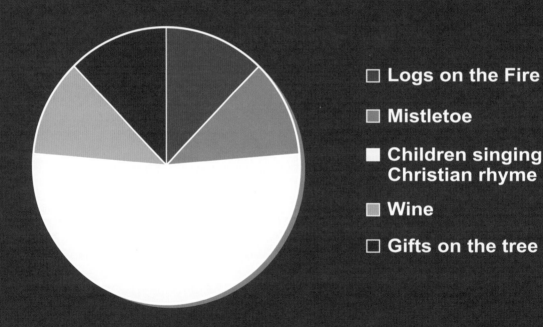

Reasons for telephonic contact

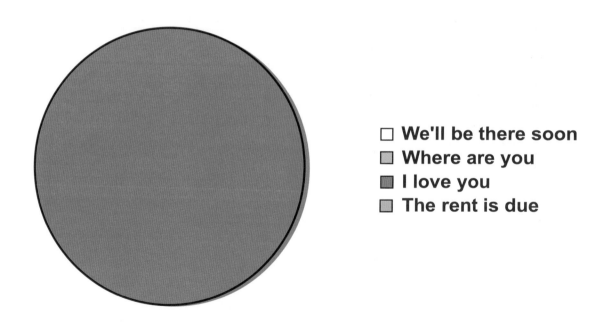

- ☐ **We'll be there soon**
- ☐ **Where are you**
- ☐ **I love you**
- ☐ **The rent is due**

Source: L Richie

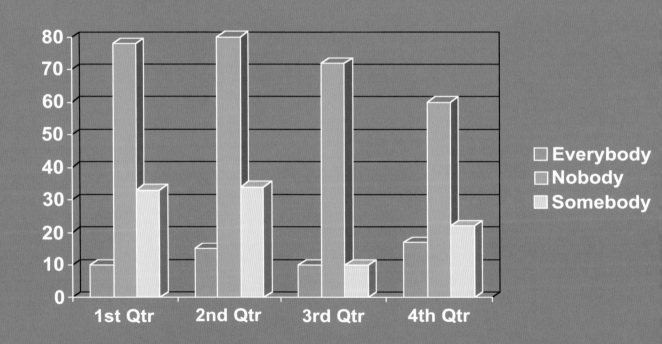

Personnel who do it better

Degrees of hurting over time

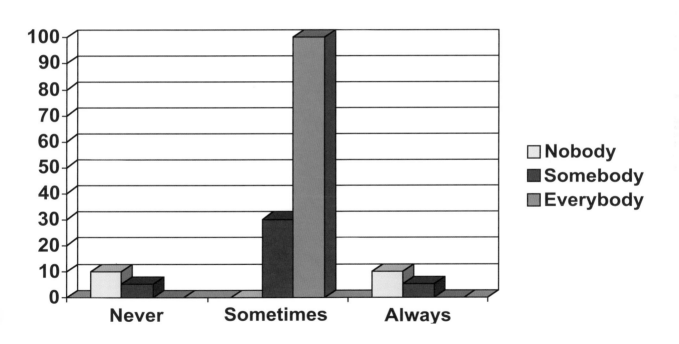

Analysis of American Girls

Emotional attributes of Kajagoogoo

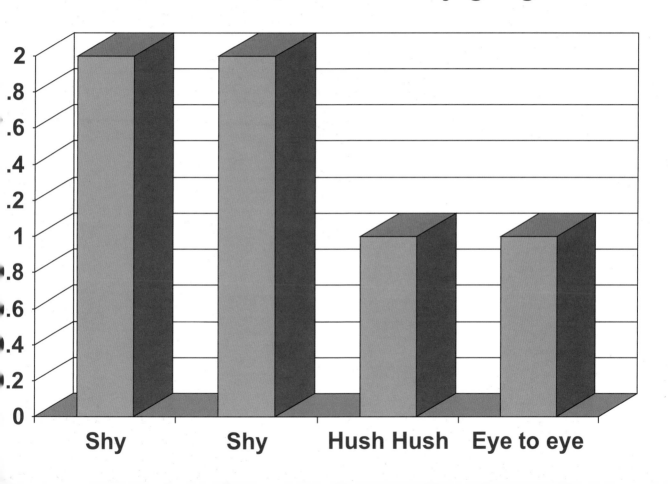

Relative conflict-based score accumulation

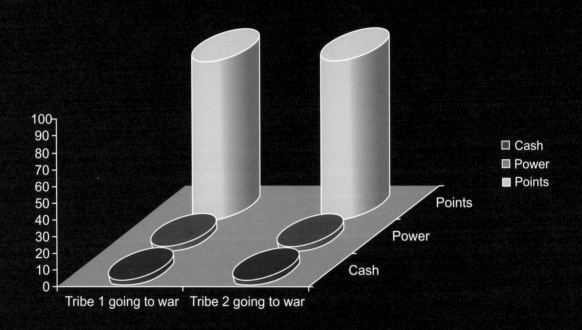

Ranking of women by name and positive disposition of reporter

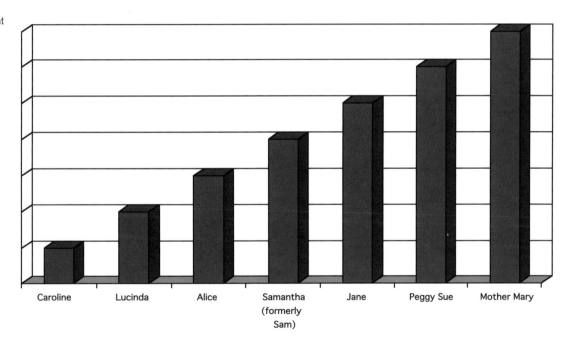

Constituant elements of Verve symphony

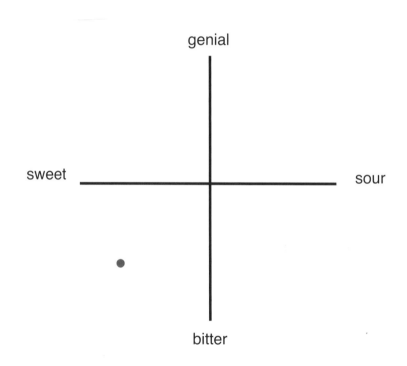

Test for familiarity with Mick Hucknall of Simply Red

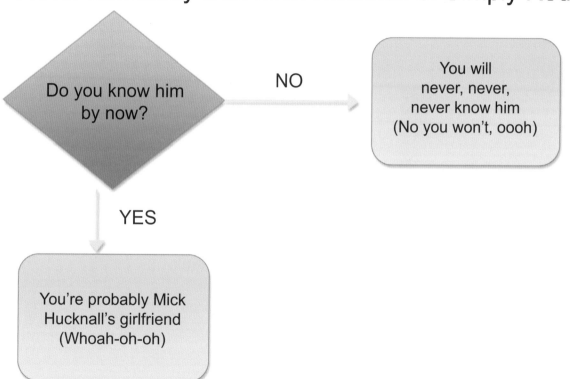

Reasons I love you

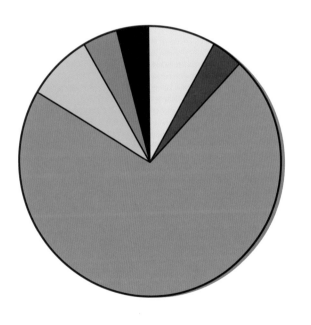

☐ You amaze me

■ You're my landlord

☐ You pay my rent

☐ You're my mother

■ I'm co-dependent

■ You're a nobel prize
winning physicist

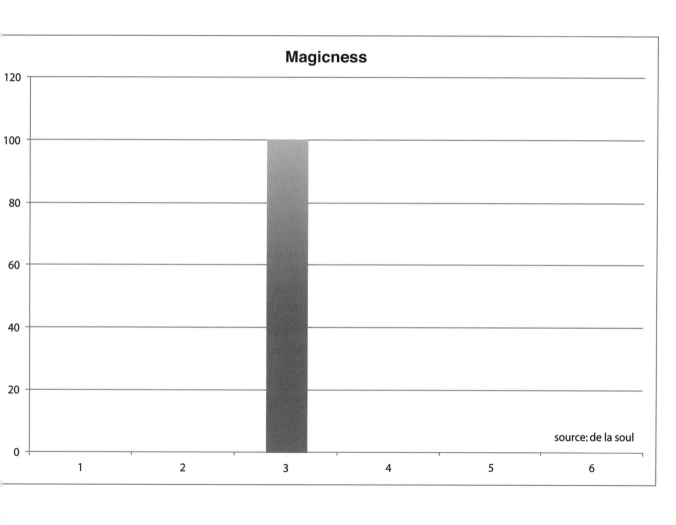

Magicness

source: de la soul

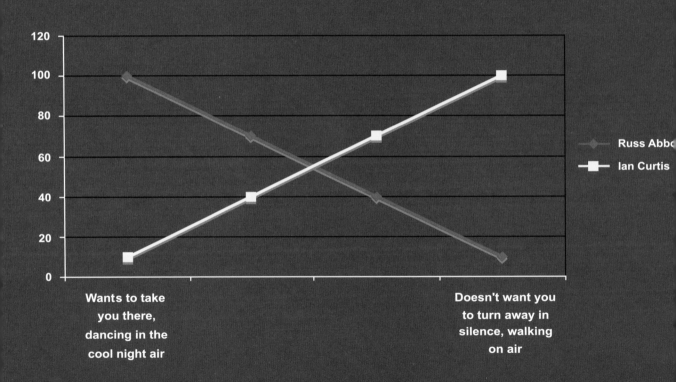

Craig David's Wall Planner

MONDAY	TUESDAY	WEDNESDAY	THURSDAY	FRIDAY	SATURDAY	SUNDAY
					2pm: Make love	
		3pm: Make love				
			5pm: Make love			
	6pm: Take her for a drink					CHILL
				8pm: Make love		
		10PM: Make love				
	11PM: Make love					

M.C. Hammer contact allowance

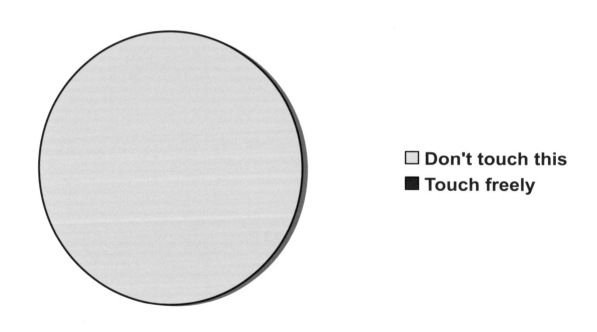

☐ **Don't touch this**
■ **Touch freely**

James Brown's Dilemma

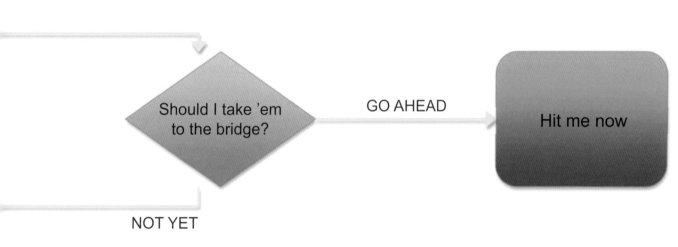

Cohen directives to creating deity-worthy tunes despite baffledness

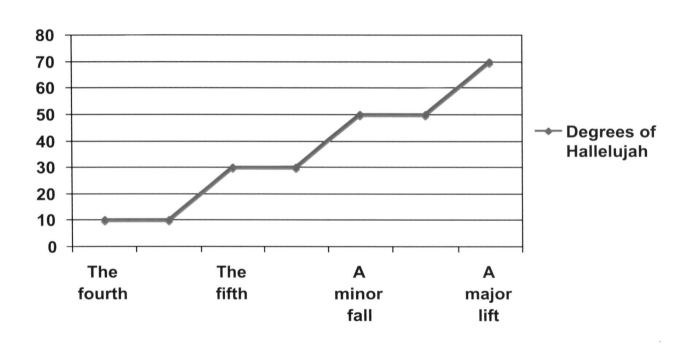

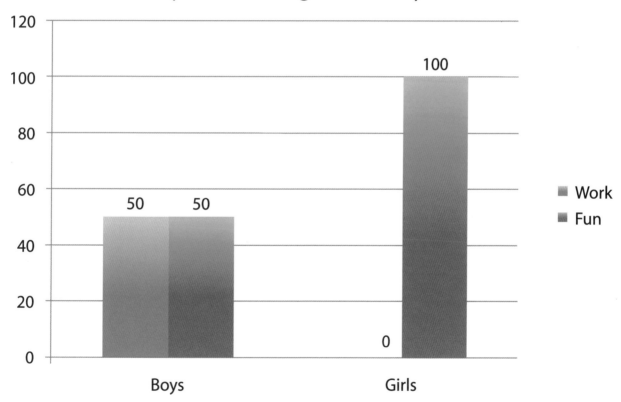

Purpose of visit
(% showing interest)

Source: C Lauper

Fox identification elements

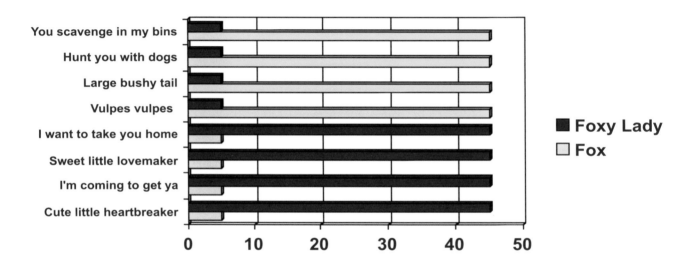

Checklist of completed work on Shakin' Stevens' ole house

Fixing shingles ☐

Fixing floor ☐

Oiling hinges ☐

Mending windowpane ☐

Proposal for falling down at your door

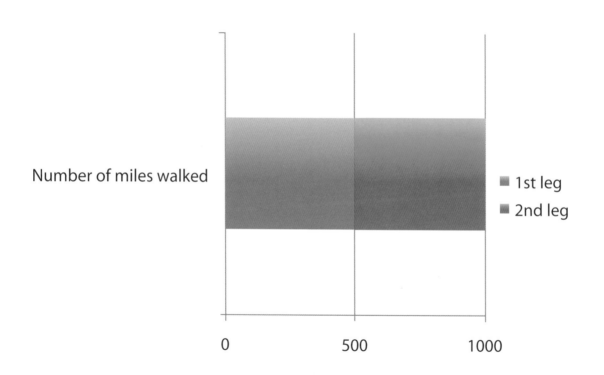

Items costed against grandfather's sweat

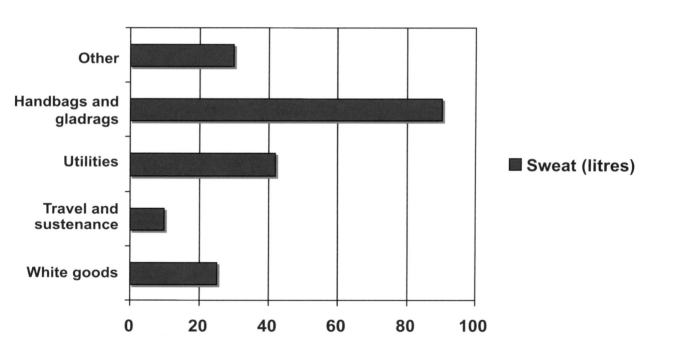

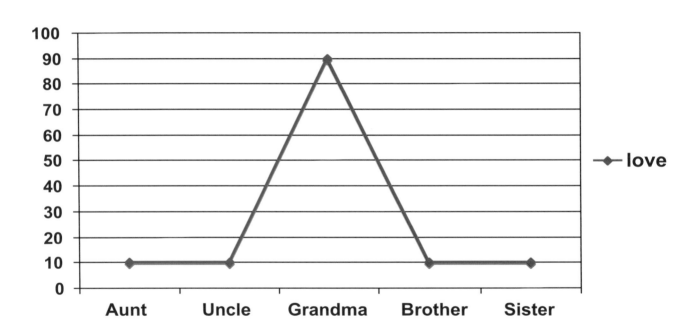

% preference of family members in the 5-10 year age group

Events leading to Police restraining order

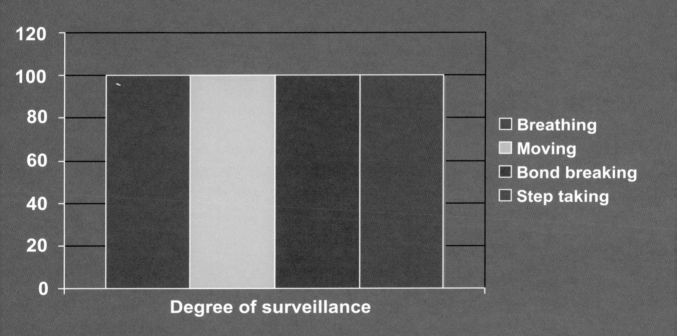

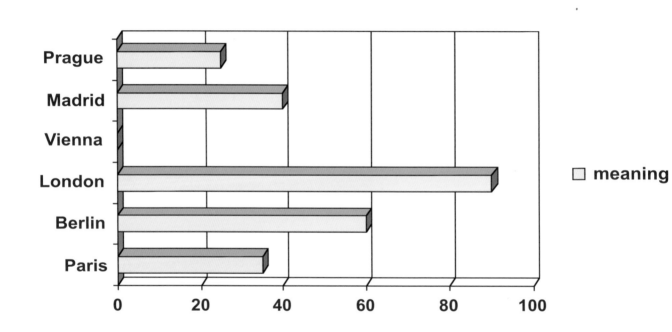

Midge Ure's feedback on European cities

Starship foundations for urban (specifically city) building preferences

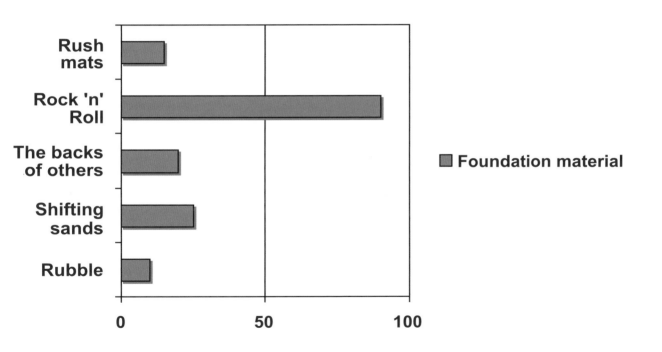

Breakdown of possible destinations following my challenge to the mighty titan and his troubadours

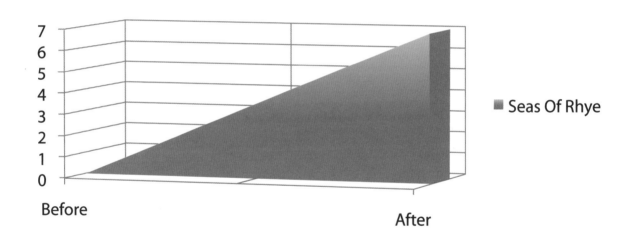